SABRINA FISHER REECE

Become Your Own Cheerleader

Moving Forward in Life Without The Support of Others

First published by In59Seconds Publiching 2026

Copyright © 2026 by SaBrina Fisher Reece

All rights reserved. No part of this publication may be reproduced, stored or transmitted in any form or by any means, electronic, mechanical, photocopying, recording, scanning, or otherwise without written permission from the publisher. It is illegal to copy this book, post it to a website, or distribute it by any other means without permission.

SaBrina Fisher Reece asserts the moral right to be identified as the author of this work.

SaBrina Fisher Reece has no responsibility for the persistence or accuracy of URLs for external or third-party Internet Websites referred to in this publication and does not guarantee that any content on such Websites is, or will remain, accurate or appropriate.

Designations used by companies to distinguish their products are often claimed as trademarks. All brand names and product names used in this book and on its cover are trade names, service marks, trademarks and registered trademarks of their respective owners. The publishers and the book are not associated with any product or vendor mentioned in this book. None of the companies referenced within the book have endorsed the book.

First edition

This book was professionally typeset on Reedsy.
Find out more at reedsy.com

This book is for every man, woman, and child who has ever allowed someone else's silence to make them feel unworthy. For those who waited for applause that never came and questioned their value because of it. The greatest gift I can offer you is learning how to cheer for yourself. This is a skill you will need for a lifetime.

Contents

Introduction		1
1	The Day I Realized I Was Waiting on Applause	3
2	Why Some People Can't Clap for You	12
3	Don't Hold Your Breath	20
4	Your Worth Isn't Up for a Vote	26
5	Learn to Encourage Yourself	31
6	How to Stop Taking Things Personally	37
7	When they Refuse to Acknowledge You	46
8	Acknowledge The Few	52
9	When Your Validation Becomes Internal	58
10	Becoming the Voice You Needed	64
11	No Need to Confront	71
12	Standing Ovation: Live Like You Believe in You	77
About the Author		82
Also by SaBrina Fisher Reece		84

Introduction

Become Your Own Cheerleader: Moving Forward in Life Without the Support of Others is a powerful, honest guide for anyone who has ever felt unseen, unsupported, or overlooked by the very people they hoped would cheer the loudest.

In this deeply personal and transformational book, SaBrina Fisher Reece invites readers into her life story, one shaped by early abandonment, profound loss, resilience, and hard-earned self-trust. From surviving childhood trauma and the murder of the grandmother who raised her, to building businesses, writing books, and leading without consistent support, SaBrina reveals what happens when you stop waiting for applause and start standing firmly in your own worth.

This is not a book about bitterness. It is a book about liberation.

Through raw storytelling and hard truths, you will learn why some people cannot clap for you, how to stop taking silence personally, and why your worth is never up for a vote. You will discover how to release the need for validation, acknowledge the few who truly support you, and become the voice you once needed to hear from others.

Each chapter builds toward one essential truth: the most powerful support you will ever receive must come from within.

Whether you are navigating family disappointment, friendship distance, professional invisibility, or emotional independence, **Become Your Own Cheerleader** offers clarity, comfort, and courage. It teaches you how to keep going when no one is watching, how to celebrate yourself without guilt, and how to live boldly without waiting for permission.

This book is for the strong ones who got strong too early. For the ones who kept showing up. For the ones who learned how to clap for themselves.

If you are ready to stop waiting for approval and start living like you believe in you, this book is for you.

1

The Day I Realized I Was Waiting on Applause

There was a day when I finally understood something that had been shaping my entire life without my permission. I realized I was waiting on applause. Waiting on approval. I had been eagerly waiting on someone, anyone, to confirm that I mattered,I needed others to tell me that I was doing well and that I was worthy of love. That realization did not come softly. It arrived heavy, layered with memory, grief, and truth I could no longer ignore.

The need for approval does not come from nowhere. It is born somewhere specific. Mine was born in abandonment.

I was an African American little girl abandoned by her drug addicted mother. That is not a dramatic statement. It is a factual one. At three months old my mother put me into a suitcase and attempted to throw me into the ocean like trash. That is not metaphor it is a real story. When your life begins with someone trying to discard you, the world does not feel safe. Love does not feel guaranteed and your worth does not feel inherent. So you start searching for proof. Proof that you are wanted. You need proof that you do indeed belong in this world. That is what I desperately needed. Proof that I deserved to exist.

If the person who brought you into the world did not want you, where exactly are you supposed to get love from? How was I ever to know that I could be loved? Those questions haunted me long before I had language for it as a child, I did not understand abandonment intellectually. I understood it emotionally. It showed up as hyper awareness or as people pleasing and overachieving. It showed up in my life as the quiet fear that if I was not impressive enough, obedient enough, successful enough, lovable enough, I would be left again. I learned very early that applause felt like safety. Validation felt like protection. Being noticed honestly felt good to me.

After my mothers attempt to discard of me, something miraculous happened. I was rescued and I was raised by my amazing grandmother, Ella Mae Fisher Fair from Dallas, Texas. My grandmother loved me with a wholehearted and a consistent love. I never once felt unloved. She gave me a love that showed up every day no matter what. Her love was not a performance. She truly loved me and my older sister and that love was steady and strong. She fed and clothed us. She taught us how to pray and introduced us to God. She sang in church every Sunday and took us to Sunday school. She made me feel seen without requiring me to earn it. Our grandmother gave us the structured secure life that we would not have had with our mother.

My sister Mary and I were the only two children of her youngest son Jesse Paul Fisher. We knew what love felt like because of her. Our father loved us too but his love for alcohol was stronger. That consistent type of love teaches you that you are safe and valuable. It allows you just breathe and enjoy life. But it also creates a new kind of vulnerability. Because once you finally know love, the thought of losing it becomes unbearable.

And I did lose it.

My grandmother was murdered in front of me when I was seventeen years old. Yes, the beautiful woman who raised me. The woman who saved me from my mother and took me home. The only woman who was my anchor to the world. She was taken from me violently and suddenly by our grandfather, her husband of thirty-two years.

That was the day my life changed. I was right there. I saw it all. He killed her with one gun shot womb to the head. My life was never the same after that. The sweet, pure consistently love was gone. The timing made it even more devastating. Thirty days after I graduated from Centennial High School in Compton, California, the ground beneath my feet disappeared. I had to get up, walk the stage for high school graduation and somehow begin my life.

I had just crossed one finish line, only to be thrown into grief without warning. That tragic loss shattered something inside of me. Not just emotionally, but spiritually. I had already experienced the abandonment and abuse of my mother. Now I was left alone again, this time after believing I was safe. That kind of loss does something to a person. It teaches you that love is temporary. That safety is fragile and there is no room for trust. It made me realize that I was alone in a huge world with people capable of doing horrendous things. My mother was still out in the world chasing drugs. My father had died when I was ten. Who would love me now? Were would I turn for love and validation?

So I began to chase it harder.

Ironically, I went on to become a cheerleader in high school. At Centennial High School in Compton, California, I was the captain of the varsity cheerleading squad. I was a leader then long before I gained my true voice. I stood in front of crowds, smiling, rallying, encouraging, lifting the energy of everyone around me. I knew how to clap for others and I knew how to lead with enthusiasm. I knew how to motivate long before I created the #In59Seconds Movement. Life would later reveal that I was learning those skills early because one day I would need them desperately in adulthood. One day, I would need to learn how to cheer for myself.

At the time, I did not see the connection. I thought I was just motivated and busy. Just strong and determined to win. But looking back, I see it clearly. I was learning how to generate applause because I did not trust it would always come. It is sad for me when I think back but it very true. I never trust that love in any form would simply be there.

I did not realize it but I spent most of my life waiting on applause. I thought I was just a driven business owner. A motivated speaker, and a ambitious entrepreneur. I was indeed all of that but underneath was a little girl still asking the same question she had been asking since infancy. Am I enough now? Do I deserve to be loved?

Every achievement became a silent request. Every milestone became a test. Success became a performance, not because I loved attention, but because attention felt like reassurance. If people clapped, I could breathe and feel good about myself. If they noticed my achievements then I could relax. If they approved then I knew I had done well and I could rest.

But the applause never lasted, nor did they come from the

people I needed them from the most. No matter how much I accomplished, the hunger returned. No matter how much I gave, the emptiness resurfaced. People justifiably praised me, because I owned and operated the largest Braiding & Dreadlock salon in Los Angeles, Ca. I employed over 1700 young women in my salon over a 30 years period. Maintaining staffs as large as 11 girls at a time. In business I had indeed done well for myself, I deserved the praises. But that praise never reached the place inside of me that was wounded first.

Sincere applause are wonderful and can feel great but they cannot heal abandonment. It can only distract you from it. I stayed distracted for many years, until some disappointment in life would remind me that I yearned for love. I became very good at appearing strong. I learned how to smile through pain. I showed up even when I was breaking. I learned how to succeed while grieving, and the world rewarded me for it. People admired my resilience. They praised my strength. They clapped for my accomplishments. But none of them knew that every clap felt like a temporary bandage on a very old wound. I needed those band-aids and they sustained me for many years.

When you are abandoned early, you grow up believing love must be earned. You believe approval is currency. You believe being impressive is your protection. Then you sit back and wait for people to clap. You wait for people to notice. You wait for people to validate what you already know in your spirit but cannot yet feel in your body.

The day I realized I was waiting on applause was not some dramatic moment of revelation. It was quiet and It was internal. I noticed how much power I had handed over to other people's reactions. I noticed how silence made me uncomfortable. Like a two year old who needs you to clap, I needed them to immediately stoke my ego and tell me I was amazing so that I could feel it inside.

I noticed how deeply I was affected by whether or not people showed up for me emotionally. I became aware of how much of my self worth was tied to the response of others instead of truth. The truth that I was born great and worthy of love just like each of you.

The realization that I needed others to make me feel whole hurt me, because it meant I had been living from a wound instead of from wholeness. I had been asking the world to confirm something that only I could heal. Other human beings can not heal you.

I began to understand that my need for approval was not vanity. It was survival. It was the echo of a child who did not feel chosen. It was the residue of loss layered on top of loss. It was grief that had nowhere to land.

Once I saw it clearly, I could no longer un-see it. I began the slow work of separating who I was from how I was received. I began questioning why silence felt so loud to me. I began sitting with the discomfort instead of running from and suppressing it. I giving myself the reassurance I had been seeking externally my entire life.

That was not easy. It will be a process that requires commitment for anyone who begins that journey. But it is beyond worth it. Embarking upon a journey of true, authentic self love will change your life forever, as it did mine.

Healing abandonment requires grieving the childhood you did not get, the safety you did not have, and the love that should have been unconditional but was not. It requires facing the truth that no amount of applause can rewrite your beginning. Only compassion and forgiveness can.

I had to learn how to stop clapping for myself only when others were watching and build an authentic self-esteem. I had to teach myself how to validate my own existence because I mattered most. I had to learn how to tell that little girl inside of me that she did not have to perform well or rack up accomplishments to be loved anymore.

That was the beginning of becoming my own cheerleader. But before you can become your own cheerleader, you have to understand why you were waiting on applause in the first place. You have to trace it back to the moments your worth was questioned before you ever had a voice. You sincerely have to seek healing to mend those broken parts of you that prevent you from knowing you are great.

For me, it began in abandonment and deepened with loss. What started as a wound quietly grew roots, then followed me into adulthood wearing a different name. It called itself ambition. It looked like strength, hustle and resilience. But beneath it all lived a longing to be seen, a hope that someone would finally say, *I see you. I choose you. You matter.*

This pattern does not wear the same face for everyone. Sometimes it shows up as constant striving. Sometimes as over-giving. Sometimes as the endless chase for approval from people who do not know how to offer it. That is why it matters to pause long enough to recognize the behavior, not with shame, but with compassion. Because what we can name and acknowledge, we can heal. What we can see clearly, we can gently release.

You are not unfinished. You are not invisible. You are not waiting to become worthy. You are already just as valuable, just as deserving, and just as significant as the people you have been standing still for, hoping they would clap.

This chapter is not about blame. It is about awareness. Because when you understand the origin of your need for approval, you stop judging yourself for having it. You stop calling yourself weak. You stop shaming your coping mechanisms. You begin to replace survival strategies with healing ones.

The little girl who needed applause did not need more achievements. She needed safety. She needed reassurance and consistency. Stable love is what she needed.

Eventually, I had to learn to sincerely love and support myself, and that is where this journey truly begins.

SaBrina Fisher age 17 at Cheerleading Camp in 1986

2

Why Some People Can't Clap for You

There comes a moment in life when you realize something that changes everything: not everyone who loves you knows how or will choose to celebrate you. Not everyone who knows you is capable of clapping when you rise. This realization can either harden you or heal you, depending on how you understand it. Having expectations from others will cause you great pain.

For a long time, I took silence personally. Some people will not say the words you need to hear and that is OK. When I didn't receive encouragement from friends or family, I assumed it meant I wasn't doing enough. When milestones passed without acknowledgment, I believed I must not be worthy of celebration. When I shared dreams and was met with indifference or subtle discouragement, I internalized it as rejection.

What I did not understand then was that their inability to clap had nothing to do with me and everything to do with their capacity. They may not be on a journey of self discovery, so they may have no idea why they don't celebrate you. It truly may not be personal.

Some people cannot clap for you because they were never clapped for themselves. They grew up in environments where praise was scarce, where survival mattered more than celebration, where emotions were tucked away and vulnerability was considered weakness. In those spaces, achievement is often met with silence, not because it lacks value, but because joy was never modeled. When you are raised without affirmation, you don't naturally know how to give it.

Years ago, I attended an intensive five-day transformational group seminar, one of those experiences that strips titles, status, and masks away and leaves only truth in the room. What I learned there changed the way I see people forever. I learned that no matter how accomplished someone appears on the outside, many are still quietly carrying pain rooted in one simple desire: to be loved and approved of by their family.

I watched a middle-aged doctor, a man who had graduated from USC Medical School in California, a man who had done everything society says you are supposed to do to be considered "successful," break down in uncontrollable tears. Through sobs, he shared that when he finally became a doctor and proudly told his father, the only response he received was, "What's next, son?" No celebration. No acknowledgment. No moment of pride. Just a moving finish line.

Watching that man cry taught me something I will never forget: your economic status does not heal your wounds. Achievement does not automatically mend the places where love was missing. Degrees do not replace affirmation. Titles do not soothe the inner child still waiting to be seen. We are all made from pure love, and when that love is withheld, dismissed, or made conditional, something inside us fractures no matter how strong we appear.

That moment reshaped my understanding of applause. It reminded me that we should clap for people whenever we can, because we never truly know what it took for them to stand where they are. We may not know their story, but we do know we each carry one of our own, and kindness costs nothing.

At the same time, I learned another difficult truth. Some people struggle to clap not because you do not deserve it, but because your growth confronts their stagnation. It forces them to look at themselves. You being courageous becomes a mirror for them. Your momentum highlights the dreams they postponed. You were willing to try and to them, that exposes the risks they avoided. Instead of sitting honestly with that discomfort, some people protect their ego by pulling back their support from you. To them applauding you makes them feel pressure to accomplish more themselves.

It is often easier to minimize your progress than to face their own unrealized potential. It is easier to stay silent than to admit regret. But we all have regrets. It is easier to withhold encouragement than to acknowledge envy, fear, or disappointment within themselves.

This does not make them cruel. Nor does it make them a bad person. It makes them human. Once you understand that, you stop shrinking to make others comfortable. You stop chasing applause from people who are still learning how to give it. You learn to clap for yourself, not from arrogance, but from healing. You recognize that your journey deserves acknowledgment even if it comes from your own hands first.

But when you don't understand this, you will continue to bleed in places where people only have bandages for themselves.

I had to learn that silence is not always disapproval. Sometimes it is personal limitation within them that has nothing to do with you. Sometimes it is fear. Many people want more but are afraid to take that leap of faith. Some people can be jealous and not even realize it. We can all excel in all areas but the road will always be harder for the one that does not believe they can.

There were seasons where I was winning externally and breaking internally. People assumed I was always okay because I appeared strong and I was always smiling. They assumed I didn't need encouragement because I kept moving forward. They felt applauding me was unnecessary because I seemed self-sufficient and confident. What they didn't know was how much effort it took for me to stand upright while carrying invisible pain.

Some people do not clap because they think you don't need it. They assume that bright smile means certain confidence. That is not always the case. They think what they perceive as confidence is arrogance and the last thing you need is another compliment. Sometimes that is the farthest from the truth.

Many people don't clap because they have already chosen their seat at tables where your name is spoken of negatively. They have participated in secret conversations, shared side glances, and formed opinions without ever asking you how you got here or what it cost for you to stand where you stand. This is an uncomfortable truth, but it is a real one. While we cannot control those conversations, we also cannot afford to become distracted by them. Allowing their whispers to pull our focus would only slow the very progress that unsettles them.

Some people mistake resilience for invulnerability but strong people can be very vulnerable and need to be encouraged as well. They assume that because you keep going, you must not feel pain. Because you are consistent, they believe it must be easy for you. When you show up strong, they assume you do not need support. They see the results but never the sacrifice. They admire the outcome while ignoring the years of uncertainty, the sleepless nights, the private tears, and the moments you almost gave up but didn't.

They see the finished product and overlook the process. They see the light and dismiss the fire that forged it, and because they cannot see the struggle, they convince themselves that you already have everything you need. They feel you don't need there congratulations. In their minds, your strength disqualifies you from needing encouragement. Your success becomes their excuse for withholding kindness. Oh but how wrong they are. We can show up, smile on the outside while still being quite broken on the inside. Giving up is simply not an option.

This is why you must learn not to measure your worth by who claps for you. Silence does not mean you are unsupported by the universe. It simply means some people are not equipped to celebrate what they did not have the courage to pursue. Their lack of applause is not a reflection of your value. It is a reflection of their distance from their own. In those moment try to avoid taking it personal, because sometimes it might not be. Remember everyone is living a life according to their perception. There can be so many different perceptions of the exact same thing. Their living in their head and you are living in yours. We are all trying to navigate this human life experience the best we can.

This is why waiting on external validation can be so dangerous. People will often misread you. They will underestimate your need for encouragement. They will assume your strength eliminates your sensitivity. If you allow their silence to define you, you will begin to shrink parts of yourself that were never meant to be small. You can choose not to be hurt by their silence.

I had to learn that applause is a gift, not a requirement. Some people genuinely want to clap but don't know how. Others want to clap but are afraid of what it means if they do. Some simply cannot clap at all because they are still trying to survive their own unresolved pain, and that OK too.

Understanding this freed me and it will do the same for you.

It freed me from chasing reactions like a needy little puppy. It freed me from performing for validation and becoming resentful when I did not get it. Most importantly, it freed me from interpreting silence as a verdict on my worth. I now know that I am worthy even if no one cheers for me. I have now become my own cheerleader, and you should do the same.

Growth changes dynamics. When you grow internally you expect less from people. When you heal it changes your inner conversations. You become the prize, and that confidence changes your energy. You can then rise knowing that you are all you need. Working on your self-confidence disrupts the version of yourself that people were accustomed to managing. You do not need them or their applause. You can become the best version of you by clapping for yourself. Your relationship with others will change for the better when you expect noting from them. Any cheering they do for you is icing on the cake but you are the whole cake.

Your expansion can make others feel unnecessary, insecure, or exposed. This is why some people disappear when you level up. Not because you abandoned them, but because your evolution no longer fits the role they assigned you. They needed you to need them. When you began evolving you stopped being available in the same ways to them. You stop needing them to validate you. That shift can feel threatening to those who relied on your dependency.

Learning this was painful, but necessary. Because once you understand why some people can't clap for you, you stop begging them to. You stop running over to them for a pat on the head like your puppy does when you come home. You stop over explaining your dreams. You stop dimming your light to preserve their comfort. Most importantly you stop equating support with love.

Love can exist without applause, and applause can exist without love. That distinction matters. Some of the loudest claps will come from strangers who see your courage clearly. Many of the quietest responses will come from people who watched you grow up. That does not mean your journey is wrong. It means proximity sometimes blinds people to transformation.

You do not need universal approval to move forward. You simply need confidence, clarity and focus. You need self-love and trust. You must have the courage to clap for yourself when the room is quiet. Because the loudest breakthroughs often happen in silence. Be still and look in the mirror and remind yourself that YOU GOT THIS!

When you become your own cheerleader, you stop turning to others for approval. You stop waiting for them to give you permission. You no longer measure your progress by their reaction. You start living from conviction instead of applause.

Some people won't clap for you. PERIOD! It is a harsh reality. Some won't cheer no matter what. Not because you aren't worthy. But because they don't yet know how to celebrate something they haven't activated within themselves yet. They want success. They want love. They want peace but they are too afraid to go after it.

Your life does not require an audience to be meaningful. As I always say "You are Great and this is your life to Create, So Lets Go!"

3

Don't Hold Your Breath

There is a saying people often use casually, almost jokingly: *Don't hold your breath.* It usually means, don't wait too long, because you'll be waiting forever and possibly die while waiting lol. We laugh when we hear it, but hidden inside that little phrase is a serious life lesson. Holding your breath while waiting for certain people to show up for you can suffocate your spirit if you are not careful.

Too many of us spend years emotionally holding our breath. We wait for a call. We wait for acknowledgment. We wait for approval. We wait for someone to finally say, "I see you." We wait for family and friends. We sit around waiting for people who say they love us to prove it. We end up waiting so long that we forget how to breathe on our own.

Here is the hard truth most people do not want to say out loud: the people closest to you are often the ones most likely to disappoint you. Not because they are evil. Not because they do not love us or care for us at all. But because familiarity can dull appreciation, and proximity can breed comparison instead of celebration. Sometimes people were never taught how to emotionally support others. Many times people assume we already know they are proud of us. But they have never said it.

We definitely expect our family to clap first. We expect our friends to be prouder than most. We need the people who truly know us, the ones who watched us struggle to cheer the loudest when we finally win. That does not always happened, and when that does not happen, the disappointment cuts deeper than criticism from a stranger ever could. I have cried a many a tear over not receiving a simply "Congratulations" from family.

To be clear I'm not bring this up to make you angry with them. I just want you to learn how to not take it personally. I learned this lesson in a very personal way.

When my business, Braids by SaBrina, reached its fifteen year anniversary, it was a major milestone. Most small businesses do not make it that far. Fifteen years represents resilience, sacrifice, consistency, sleepless nights, risk, loss, recovery, and faith. By that point, I had employed over 1,700 women in the Los Angeles community. I had created jobs and opportunities. I had built something from nothing. I had left a mark in the world and I was proud of myself.

Even the city officials noticed and awarded me for my success. Jasmyne Cannick wrote an inspiring article about me in the Los Angeles Sentinel News Paper. I appear of Front Page and KFI Radio shows. I received letters and acknowledgments from people in positions of power. Council woman Jan Perry recognized my contribution and presented me with an award in person. Chief Bernard Parks came by to shake my hand and congratulate me on fifteen years of service to the community. I received official recognition from the city through Isadore Hall and a few other council people. These were people who did not grow up with me, who did not know my childhood pain, who had no emotional obligation to me, saw my work and honored it. I felt wonderful and accomplished and noticed.

I should have been celebrating freely. I should have been floating on cloud nine. Instead, my heart felt heavy. My sister never said congratulations. The sister I was raised with. The person whose approval had always mattered to me more than I realized. The one I subconsciously expected to see me without needing an explanation. Her silence hurt more than any criticism ever could.

That moment forced me to face something I had avoided my entire life. I was still holding my breath for validation from someone I loved. I needed it more than air.

I eventually found the courage to speak up, gently and respectfully, because that is who I am. I told her it hurt my feelings that such a major accomplishment went unacknowledged. That conversation was not about blame. It was about me finally saying, "I matter too."

That moment marked a turning point. For most of my life, I had accepted being the baby sister. We are only eleven months apart, but she was always the older one. For years, people did not even call me by my name. I was "little Mary." They did not mean harm. They did not realize the impact it left on me. But identity matters. Being constantly framed as the smaller version of someone else quietly teaches you to minimize yourself. My sister Mary is indeed brilliant and very well accomplished. If would be years before I realized I was equally as brilliant. No one should ever compare children. I know my value now and I want each of you to know yours.

Families often do this without realizing it. The first child gets named. The second child gets compared. Over time, that comparison can seep into your bones. You begin measuring your worth through someone else's shadow. You begin waiting for recognition instead of owning your presence. Maybe that is how God needed it to be so that I would go on the journey of remembering how great I was. I do know now and that is why I write books like this to encourage others.

I do not blame my sister, she was a child just like me. I don't even blame the people who called me "Lil Mary" most of my childhood. This is not about fault. This is about awareness, and we all need to wake up to our infinite potential in life. We all have our own individual purpose here.

Sometimes the people closest to us do not see us clearly because they met us before we met ourselves. They remember who we were, not who we became. They freeze us in time, while life keeps moving forward. We want them to acknowledge our progress and they may never see it. Waiting for them to catch up can keep you stuck. They may be simply trying to get their own life on track. Holding your breath waiting for applause from them can quietly suffocate your growth.

This chapter is not about resentment. It is about release. You cannot wait on others to validate what God has already confirmed. You cannot pause your purpose until someone claps. That train needs to move forward no matter what. You cannot stop moving because someone refuses to look up. More importantly, do not get upset with them or start putting yourself down if they do not give you the validation that you need.

Some people find fault in you because it feels safer than trying. themselves. They critique others because courage intimidates them. Some people withhold praise because it forces them to confront what they have not been brave enough to do.

That is not your burden to carry. You must live for you and

you alone. You must learn to breathe without permission from others. You uplift and encourage yourself. Male or female it does not matter. You must become your own strongest support system.

I stopped waiting for people to notice me. I stopped internalizing silence. I stopped assuming lack of support meant lack of worth. I stopped measuring my success by who showed up for me, and realized I am enough all by myself. So are each and every one of you.

You have to decide at some point that your life is too important to be lived on pause. Your dreams are too expensive to be funded by someone else's approval. Your future is too big and bright to be dependent on someone else's encouragement.

Do not hold your breath waiting for family and friends to understand and support you. Do not hold your breath waiting for friends and family to cheer for you. Do not hold your breath waiting for recognition from people who benefit from you staying small.

Be Still and close your eyes, take a deep breath and smile for the person that you are today. Give yourself a big hug and clap for yourself.

There will be people who never acknowledge your growth. and you can not continue to allow that to be a source of pain. There will be people who change the subject when you share good news. There will be people who find something negative to say instead of celebrating your progress. These people will always exist. Let them be and limit their access to you. Their silence is not your sentence.

Your job is not to convince anyone that your accomplishments matter. Your job is to live in a way that honors your effort, your faith, and your evolution. We were put here on this beautiful earth to live, love and learn. No ones life is the same. All of our experiences will be different. Always be the supportive person that you want others to be. Do not become angry and bitter.

I will be encouraging people with the #In59Seconds Movement for the rest of my life, because the world needs it. If we all take a minimum of 59 seconds a day to uplift, motivate and encourage ourselves and another human being we can have a better world.

4

Your Worth Isn't Up for a Vote

For a long time, I lived as if my worth needed confirmation. As if it required someone else to aggree. I needed to be validated by applause, approval, or acceptance from the people around me. I did not consciously think this way, but my behavior told the truth. I waited for reactions. I watched faces. I listened for praise. I measured myself by how others responded to my wins, my growth, and even my pain.

What I did not recognize back then is that when you allow other people to vote on your value, you will always live at the mercy of their limitations. You don't need that. I do understand why we all desire it but we do not need it to succeed.

Your worth is not a group decision. You were born valuable and worthy. It is not determined by consensus. It is a fact for us all. Sometimes when people climb the ladder of success they forget that God does not love them more or less because of their economic status. We are all the same in Gods eyes. That fact keeps me humble. No matter what I accomplish, I am no better that anyone else.

Your worth is intrinsic. It was assigned at birth. It came with your first breath. It is not negotiable. Man, woman, boy or girl we are valuable pieces to this human puzzle. We may express our gifts differently but we all have them.

Most of us are never taught this. Society make you believe that there is a human hierarchy. Dispelling that belief is a huge step in your spiritual evolution.

We are taught to perform well to be loved, to behave well to be accepted, succeed to be respected. Somewhere along the way, worth becomes conditional. Once worth begins to feels conditional, we start auditioning for love instead of standing in truth and confidence.

I spent many years unconsciously auditioning. Auditioning for approval from family. Auditioning for affirmation from partners. Auditioning for recognition from people who had no authority over my life but plenty of influence over my emotions.

I can remember wanting to be liked in a few organizations I was a member of. By then i was out in the world changing lives. I was writing self-help books, speaking motivationally and running a successful business yet only a handful of people ever acknowledged me. What I have since learned is: that handful is enough. Appreciate them and do not focus on the others. Trust me they see you.

I remember running around many rooms complimenting others, trying to make sure they felt good about themselves. It is natural for me to intentionally bring a smile to the face of others. I would dim my light and shrink in rooms where I knew I was meant to expand. But that didn't last long because it is so far from who I am. I enjoy shining like a star. I understand that part of my purpose is to make others feel that way too.

I know my value now and here is the truth that I had to learn the hard way: not everyone will see your value, and that does not mean it is not there. People will be impressed by you and never say it. Do not internalize that and start questioning yourself.

Some people just cannot clap for you because doing so would require them to confront their own stagnation. A lot of people withhold validation because it threatens the story they tell themselves about you. Many people are more comfortable when you remain familiar, predictable, and smaller than your potential. Let those days be over and rise and become the person God intended you to be.

We live in a world with people, so I understand the need for their input but we must get to a point in life where we know that their opinions are irrelevant to our worth. We are all valuable beings. Living this life trying to figure it out and have the best life experience we can. No longer allow yourself to focus on the non-support of others. Become so engulfed in gratitude for the few that do love and support you that you do not even notice the ones that don't.

When I finally began to understand this, my entire emotional posture changed. I stopped waiting to be chosen. I stopped running around the room kissing people butts so they would like me. I stopped down playing my success to make others feel better. I stopped seeking permission to take up space. I stopped apologizing for my ambition, my healing, my growth, and my confidence. I put myself first and learned how to *"Become My Own Cheerleader"*

I realized something profound: people can only meet you as deeply as they have met themselves. If someone has not done the work, they will not know how to honor someone who has. If someone is afraid to evolve, they will resist celebrating your evolution. If someone benefits from you doubting yourself, they will never encourage you to stand tall.

That is why your worth cannot be placed in the hands of others. You re in charge of it, so you must work on developing and authentic self-esteem. Your confidence need to be real not a facade.

The moment you decide that your value does not require approval, you become emotionally free. You stop chasing validation and start cultivating alignment. You stop reacting to the silence of others and start responding to your truth. You are a phenomenal creation of God so stop asking, "Why didn't they show up for me?" and start asking, "What kind of life do I want to build regardless?"

This shift is not easy. It requires courage and a lot of inner work. It requires authentic self love and trust. It requires you to sit with the discomfort of disappointing people who are used to you seeking their approval. The only approval you need is yours. You are qualified to make good decisions and celebrate the success of those decisions by yourself if you have to.

But on the other side of that discomfort is peace. I had to learn that being misunderstood does not make you wrong. Being unsupported does not make you unworthy. Being overlooked does not make you invisible. It simply means you are no longer operating at the level of a person who need consensus to feel safe. You are now your best friend. You are now your whole team. Mind, Body and Spirit.

Some of the most powerful people you will ever meet learned early how to validate themselves. They do not wait for applause to move forward. They do not retreat because someone disagrees or does not *see* them. They do not prove their worth to people committed to misunderstanding them. They trust their choices and inner knowing.

That is what I was so thrilled to finally find in myself. That is what I want for you. I want you to understand that your worth is not up for debate. You are Great and there is no doubt about that. I now have a self esteem that does not rise and fall based on who claps, who calls, who supports, or who stays silent. You can have that too. You do not need a panel of judges to confirm what God already established.

Once you accept this, you move differently. You speak differently. You choose differently. You stop negotiating with people who cannot meet you where you are headed.

You stop holding your breath waiting on others and you finally exhale into the life you were always meant to live.

5

Learn to Encourage Yourself

There came a point in my life when I realized something that changed everything: encouragement is not something we should wait for. It is something we must learn to generate from within. That understanding didn't arrive overnight. It came through years of disappointment, silence, unmet expectations, and learning the hard way that the world does not always shoe up for you when you need it to. Sometimes the room is quiet. Sometimes the people you thought would cheer don't show up, and sometimes, the only voice you will hear is your own. this book will teach you that your own voice is more that enough.

That is why learning to encourage yourself is not optional. It is essential. It is my personal belief that a simple 59 seconds of positivity, kindness, and love each day can tangibly change the course of our lives. I know that sounds almost too simple, but transformation does not always come from massive, dramatic moments. Often, it comes from small, intentional choices repeated consistently. Whether we give those 59 seconds to ourselves or to another human being, the impact is equally powerful.

There are days when life hits us hard. Days when you feel overlooked, misunderstood, underappreciated, or exhausted from trying. Days when you look around for encouragement and realize there is no one there. No phone call. No text. No applause. No reassurance. Those are the moments when learning how to motivate and inspire yourself becomes one of the most valuable skills you will ever develop.

This is not about becoming emotionally hardened or pretending you don't need support. It is about becoming emotionally equipped. It is about building an inner foundation that does not collapse when the outside world is quiet. When you learn to encourage yourself, you become less dependent on external validation and more grounded in internal truth. You stop shrinking when others don't see you. You stop questioning your worth when others fail to acknowledge your effort.

Because life is fast. It moves quickly. Responsibilities pile up. Time feels scarce. Between work, family, obligations, and survival, many of us feel like we don't have the luxury to focus on personal development. We tell ourselves we'll get to it later. When things slow down. When life is easier. When someone finally notices how hard we're trying.

But I believe personal development does not require hours of solitude or perfect conditions. I believe it starts with something much smaller and much more accessible. I believe if we can commit to simple gestures of encouragement, even for just 59 seconds a day, we can make a meaningful difference in our own lives and in the lives of others.

That belief is what led me to create the **#In59Seconds** movement which i speak about briefly in a earlier chapter.

In 2018, I created #In59Seconds to teach people that no matter how busy you are, committing to a minimum of 59 seconds a day to uplift, motivate, and encourage yourself and another human being can dramatically improve your quality of life. Not tomorrow. Not someday. Today. We all need motivation. Men, woman and children can all benefit from the #In59SecondsMovement.

I wish I had learned this lesson earlier in life. I wish I had known the importance of uplifting myself when I was a young woman. It would not have taken me a lifetime to learn my value. It would not have taken so long to understand that waiting on others to affirm me was costing me years of joy. I can't live in regret nor can I turn back the hands of time, but I can spend the rest of my life making sure others understand the importance of self motivation.

Learning to encourage yourself does not mean ignoring pain. It means meeting yourself in it. It means choosing to speak life into your own spirit instead of replaying the negative voices that once made you feel small. It means standing in the mirror and telling yourself, "I am amazing," even when you don't fully believe it yet. Those are the times when you need it most.

There is something powerful about repetition. When you say something often enough, your mind begins to listen. When you speak to yourself with kindness consistently, your nervous system starts to relax. Your confidence starts to rebuild. Your posture even changes. Energy begins to shift all around you. You start making better decisions, and you stop abandoning yourself emotionally.

Standing in front of a mirror and telling yourself, "I am amazing," repeatedly until you begin to believe it can change the direction of your life. It can give you the empowerment needed to inspire others without emptying yourself in the process. Encouragement does not have to come from a crowd. It can come from your commitment to yourself.

What's beautiful about encouragement is that it multiplies. Whether it is in our homes, the workplace, churches, clubs, or any organization we may be a part of, a compliment, a handshake, or a warm, genuine hug can change the entire dynamic between people. Taking time to express positive feelings and verbally acknowledge appreciation creates emotional safety. It builds trust. It softens tension and reminds people that they matter.

We never truly know what someone is carrying. People walk into rooms with invisible battles every single day. Financial stress. Grief. Trauma. Fear. Self-doubt. Loneliness. Your encouraging words or your pleasant smile could be the very thing that keeps someone from giving up that day. I've seen it happen and I've definitely felt it myself.

Think about a time when someone made you feel seen. A moment when someone spoke hope into your life when you felt hopeless. Most of us remember those moments forever. Yet, we often underestimate our own ability to be that person for ourselves and for others.

The dynamic of so many relationships could improve if we simply took the time to verbalize appreciation. A cheerful "Good morning" in the workplace can change the tone of an entire day. Telling a coworker you're glad to see them. Letting your boss know you appreciate their leadership. Acknowledging effort instead of only pointing out mistakes.

Taking 59 seconds to turn to your children in the car on the way to school and tell them they are brilliant and capable can shape their confidence for life. Those words don't disappear when they get older. They become part of their internal dialogue. They become the voice they hear when they are afraid, unsure, or standing alone.

Encouragement strengthens then and builds identity. That is why learning to encourage yourself matters so deeply. Because once you master it internally, you no longer need permission to feel worthy. You no linger need the cheers of others. You stop outsourcing your self-esteem and waiting for someone else to validate what God already placed inside you.

There was a time in my life when I didn't know how to do this. I looked outward for reassurance. I wanted people to tell me I was doing enough. I wanted someone to notice my effort and tell me that they were proud of me. I wanted confirmation that I was on the right path. When it didn't come, I internalized the silence as rejection and I allowed it to cause me deep pain.

What I didn't understand then was that encouragement is not something you earn from others. It is something you practice within yourself. You come first. you are no good to others if you feel horrible about yourself. Build yourself up from the inside out, then go an teach it to others.

When we serve others, we serve ourselves. Encouragement flows both ways. When you uplift someone else, you strengthen the part of you that believes in goodness. You reinforce the idea that kindness matters. That words matter. That presence matters.

This is why the #In59Seconds practice works. It is small enough to be doable, but powerful enough to be transformative. It doesn't overwhelm you. It invites you.

Just 59 seconds. Fifty-nine seconds to speak life. Fifty-nine seconds to pause and breathe. Fifty-nine seconds to choose encouragement over criticism. Fifty-nine seconds to remind yourself that you are still here, still trying, still worthy.

When these moments become habitual, something shifts in

you reality. You begin to show up differently. You stop waiting on rescue. You stop holding your breath for approval. You become your own cheerleader.

I truly believe that if more of us committed to this practice, we would see a more compassionate, emotionally healthy, productive world. A world where people feel less invisible. A world where self-worth is not dependent on applause.

Encouragement is not a luxury. It is a necessity. Learning to encourage yourself is one of the greatest acts of self-respect you will ever commit to. It is how you survive seasons of silence. It is how you keep going when support is absent. It is how you stay rooted when life is uncertain.

You deserve to hear kind words. If no one else is saying them yet, you must still say them consistently to yourself anyway. Say them until you believe them. That is how lives change.

6

How to Stop Taking Things Personally

There was a time in my life when the silence of others felt like rejection. If someone didn't respond, didn't acknowledge me, didn't celebrate me, or didn't show up the way I hoped, I immediately assumed it meant something about me. I replayed conversations in my mind. I questioned my worth. I wondered what I did wrong. I made up stories in my head during moments when I was still and quiet. We cause ourselves unnecessary suffering with the stories we make up in our heads.

What I didn't understand then is something I know deeply now. Most things we take personally have absolutely nothing to do with us. For example: If we walk in a room and we hear whispers.

We do not know what people are actually saying. So why choose to think the worst. they could be saying "She is beautiful our her outfit is amazing." But we see the stares and hear the whispers and automatically start that deeply ingrained self-sabotage. We tell ourselves they are saying "Wow she has gained a little weight of what is wrong with her hair." All that could be the farthest from the truth. Since you do not and probably will never know what people are saying. You paint the picture. You design the moment the way that makes you feel best about yourself. Stop taking peoples stares and whispers personally because you are only hurting yourself when you do.

Silence is one of the most misunderstood experiences in human relationships. We interpret it as dismissal, lack of care, jealousy, disapproval, or indifference. But more often than not, silence is simply the sound of someone else dealing with their own internal world. Their fears and insecurities. Their exhaustion or unhealed wounds. They may be distracted and have no idea what you need from them at that moment.

People are carrying far more than they let on. Everyone lives in their own reality. One of the most life-changing lessons I ever learned came from a book by Don Miguel Ruiz called *The Four Agreements*. One agreement in particular shifted how I move through the world: **Do not take things personally.** That single idea altered my emotional landscape. It didn't make me cold or disconnected. It made me free.

Before that, I believed other people's reactions were reflections of my value. I thought they were intentionally ignoring my success. I believed their silence was commentary on my worth. I believed their lack of encouragement meant I wasn't doing enough with my life. Maybe this abandoned child wasn't good enough, wasn't lovable enough. But what I learned is this: people can not be given the power to control how you feel about yourself. The only head you can get inside of and assess is your own.

When someone does not clap for you, it is rarely because you don't deserve applause. It is often because they have not learned how to clap for themselves, so how can they clap for you.

Most people are quietly battling self-doubt. They are questioning their own choices. They are measuring themselves against others. Which is somethings we have all done but should stop. We have all had some degree of fear of failing. So move forward and many allow that fear to stop them in their tracks. A lot of people are afraid of trying again. When you step forward and grow, when you build, when you shine brightly, it can activate insecurities in people who are still standing still. Do not let that stop you, but do not depend on them to keep going. They are not your fuel, you are.

That silence is not an evaluation of you. It is a reflection of them, so do not take it to heart. There were seasons when I wanted people to see how hard I was trying. Absolutely, I did. It is normal to want to be acknowledged for your accomplishments. I wanted acknowledgment for my effort, my resilience, my perseverance. I wanted reassurance that I was on the right path. When it didn't come, I felt invisible. I felt dismissed and devalued.

What I didn't realize was that many of the people I expected encouragement from were emotionally overwhelmed themselves. They were struggling with their own un-met dreams. some were so busy creating like me that they rarely look up to notice me. People in this world have their own disappointments. Their own sense of inadequacy at times. They didn't have the capacity to pour into me because they were running on empty themselves. When you look at it from that angle, you stop thinking that its an intentional slight.

Silence is often not the purposeful cruelty we think it is. Learning this did not excuse hurtful behavior, but it helped me stop internalizing it. It allowed me to separate my worth from other people's emotional availability. That distinction saved me years of unnecessary suffering and it will do the same for you.

When you take things personally, you give other people authority over your inner peace. You let their mood, their attention, their response dictate how you feel about yourself. You shrink when they are quiet. You grow anxious when they are distant. You wait for them to confirm what you should already know. You are a magnificent being. We all are, no matter what stage of development we are in. We are all great and have something to contribute to this world.

Expecting someone to elevate you emotionally is a heavy burden to place on anyone. It's not truly fair. That's why a lot of marriages end, because one partner expects the other to complete them emotionally, when that is something only you can do for yourself.

A relationship can be a beautiful support system, but it was never meant to be your life support. Your partner can love you, encourage you, and stand beside you, but they cannot become responsible for regulating your emotions, healing your wounds, or filling every empty space inside you. When we place that kind of weight on another person, we don't just overwhelm them, we quietly set ourselves up for disappointment, because no human being can meet a need that was meant to be met from within.

That's where emotional maturity begins: learning how to soothe yourself, strengthen yourself, so you show up to love as a whole person, not as someone begging for love to fix what you won't face. When you learn how to elevate yourself emotionally, love becomes a choice instead of a rescue mission, and your relationship becomes a partnership instead of a pressure chamber. In line with the title of this book, a great partner can join the cheering squad, but they can never be the head cheerleader, that's your job. You lead the charge on all the cheers in your life.

Here's what I mean: a healthy partner will clap for you,

encourage you, and even grab the megaphone when you're tired. They'll show up in the stands when it matters, bring water when you're weak, and remind you of your strength when you forget. They can chant your name, celebrate your wins, and stand beside you through losses. But they cannot carry the entire spirit of your life on their shoulders. They cannot be the one responsible for keeping your hope alive, your confidence standing, and your inner fire lit every single day.

Because the truth is, when you make someone else the head cheerleader of your life, you hand them your emotional power. You start waiting for their mood to set your mood. Their words become your fuel. Their attention becomes your assurance. When they're distracted, exhausted, imperfect, or simply human, as we all are, you feel yourself dropping, not because your life is falling apart, but because you built your emotional foundation on someone else's energy.

But when you become your own head cheerleader, everything changes. You stop needing permission to believe in yourself. You stop requiring constant applause to keep going. You learn how to coach your own heart through disappointment, how to speak life over yourself when you feel low, and how to get back up without needing someone to drag you. You become the one who starts the chant, sets the rhythm, and keeps the faith, even on the days your voice shakes.

That's not being selfish. That is strength and wholeness. That's how love stays healthy, because now your partner isn't responsible for completing you, they get to complement you. They don't have to carry you, they get to stand with you. They're not pressured to fix what you haven't healed, they're free to simply love you while you keep growing.

So yes, let them join your cheering squad. Let them celebrate you. Let them support you. Let them love you loudly. But never forget: the head cheerleader of your life is you. You lead the charge. You set the tone. You decide what you believe about yourself, and when you learn how to cheer for you first, you stop chasing love to fill you up, and you start building a life that love can happily join.

The truth is, no one wakes up thinking about us the way we think they do. Most people are consumed with their own thoughts, fears, schedules, responsibilities, and struggles. Their silence is often about survival, not judgment.

Once I truly understood that, something shifted in me. I stopped chasing validation. I stopped explaining myself unnecessarily. I stopped filling in the blanks of silence with self-criticism. I learned to let quiet moments remain quiet without assigning a negative meaning to them. That is emotional maturity.

Silence does not always require interpretation. Sometimes it simply requires acceptance. I write books because I want to pass on the wisdom that I had to learn the hard way, and possibly make it easier for someone else. I want people to understand earlier in life, what took me years to grasp. I want you to know that you are not flawed because someone didn't respond. You are not unworthy because someone didn't show enthusiasm. You are not invisible because someone didn't say congratulations. Yes it feels good when all of those things happen. However we need to learn to be the source of generating that amazing feelings within ourselves.

You are still you, with or without their acknowledgment. There are people who genuinely care about you but don't know how to express it. There are people who admire you but feel intimidated by your growth. There are people who love you but are too distracted by their own pain to show up consistently. Lets release them of that responsibility. There are people who simply do not have the emotional tools to support anyone, including themselves. Say and kind word to them and move forward.

When you stop taking what people say and don't say personally, you reclaim your power. You no longer wait for permission to move forward. You stop shrinking your joy to make others comfortable. You stop interpreting quiet as rejection and start seeing it as neutral.

This does not mean you stop caring. It means you stop bleeding emotionally over things that were never meant to wound you.

There was a time when I would send a message and stare at my phone, wondering why it wasn't answered. I would replay conversations, searching for something I said wrong. I would sit in unnecessary anxiety, creating stories that lived only in my imagination.

Now, I understand that silence is not a verdict. It is not a sentence. It is not a judgment. It is simply absence of sound. When someone does not encourage you, it does not mean you are not doing something remarkable. It may mean they do not know how to encourage. When someone does not celebrate you, it does not mean your milestone is insignificant. It may mean they are struggling to celebrate themselves and you simply are not their priority right now, and that's OK.

Your job is not to fix anyone but yourself. You make sure to continue becoming who God intended you to be. When you release the need for external affirmation, your confidence becomes quieter but stronger. You stop announcing yourself loudly in every room. You stop explaining your growth and proving that you matter. You stop justifying your journey. You move with certainty because you are no longer waiting for applause. You become stable within yourself. You know you matter.

That is when you become unstoppable. Other peoples silence stops being painful when you stop needing them to make you feel good about yourself. Some of the most powerful seasons of growth happen in stillness. No audience. No recognition. No validation. Just you, your purpose, and your commitment to keep going. Those are the seasons that build character. Those are the seasons that prepare you for rooms you have not entered yet. They prepare you for Greatness!

People often celebrate the finished product but never see the silent process that created it. God works deeply in silence. Seeds grow underground. Strength is developed privately. Confidence is formed internally before it ever shows externally. Silence is not absence of progress. It is often proof of it.

When you stop taking silence personally, you give yourself emotional freedom. You no longer attach your self-worth to other people's reactions. You no longer hand your peace to people who may not know how to hold it.

You begin to understand that your value is intrinsic. It does not rise or fall based on who claps, who calls, who click "Like", who comments, or who notices.

You are enough whether the room is loud or quiet, full or empty. This chapter is an invitation to release the habit of self-blame. To stop assuming silence means you have failed. To stop believing you must be seen to be significant. You matter even when no one is watching.

When the right people arrive, they will see you clearly. Not because you demanded it, but because you never stopped being yourself. *Become your own Cheerleader.* Turn inward and encourage yourself.

That is the freedom that comes from not taking things personally. That is how you keep moving forward, even when the world is quiet.

SaBrina Fisher age 17 years old... Varsity Cheerleading Captain for Centennial High School in Compton Ca 1987

7

When they Refuse to Acknowledge You

There is a particular kind of pain that comes not from strangers, but from spaces you committed to with your whole heart. Places you believed in. Communities you showed up for year after year. Rooms you entered with sincerity, loyalty, and purpose, only to realize that no matter how much you grew, no matter how much you contributed, no matter how much impact you made, you were never truly seen.

I know that pain very well. For many years, I have been a member of a nationwide organization that I joined out of genuine passion. I did not join for recognition. I did not join to climb social ladders. I joined because the mission mattered to me. I joined because it represented something deeper than networking or status. I joined because my grandmother, Ella Mae Fair, the woman who raised me, protected me, and poured love into me daily, was a proud member. Being part of that organization felt like honoring her legacy. It felt personal. It felt sacred.

What I did not anticipate was how invisible I would become simply because I did not fit into the "in crowd." it should be against the rule to form cliques in organizations like these but it is not. I have never been one to fit into clique. Especially if I could clearly see the people clearly and opening doing things that went against the rules they took vows to uphold.

Over the years, I wrote books. I built businesses. I began motivational speaking. I impacted lives. I created movements. I changed lives. I showed up consistently, and yet, in that particular sector, acknowledgment seemed to be reserved for those who knew how to play the social game, follow the hierarchy, and blend into the culture of approval.

That has never been who I am. Nope not me. I also was one to call people out on bad behavior which never went over too well lol.

I am a strong woman. I am a leader by nature. I am a Leo Alpha female who does not shrink to fit into rooms that require silence in exchange for acceptance. I am not a follower. I do not attach myself to tables simply because familiar faces are sitting there. I am comfortable standing alone. I am comfortable sitting alone. I am comfortable being myself even when it makes others uncomfortable.

For that, I was quietly sidelined. There is something deeply unsettling about realizing that in some spaces, your authenticity is a liability. That your independence is misunderstood. Your strength and confidence is perceived as threat and your refusal to conform becomes a reason to overlook you. Until they need a monetary donation of course.

At first, it hurt more than I wanted to admit. I would attend events and watch the same people be acknowledged over and over, while my contributions went unmentioned. I would sit in rooms filled with people who knew my work, knew my impact, and yet chose silence. Not because they didn't see me, but because I wasn't part of the inner circle. I wasn't playing the game. Some would come a whisper how proud of me they were in my ear but never a public acknowledgment.

I want to be very clear here. There were individuals within that organization who loved me deeply. People I bonded with genuinely. People who saw me, supported me, and valued me. I hold those relationships with gratitude and respect. They will always matter. They are as authentic as authentic can be. They are priceless.

But the larger system was different. In the broader structure, acknowledgment was selective. Recognition was political. Visibility was conditional, and that is a difficult truth to swallow when you join something with pure intentions.

There were moments when I questioned myself. Moments when I wondered if I should soften my personality. Sit at tables I didn't belong at. Laugh at jokes I didn't find funny. Shrink my voice. Become more agreeable. Become more palatable. Nope not me. Every time I considered that, something deeper in me refused to comply.

I did not build my life by following crowds. I did not survive my childhood by blending in. I did not overcome trauma, loss, and abandonment by seeking approval. I learned early how to stand on my own, even when it was uncomfortable.

So I stayed. I refused to leave the organization, not out of stubbornness, but out of purpose. I joined for a reason greater than recognition. I joined because of legacy. I joined because of belief. I joined because they did not get to run me off simply because I did not fit into their social structure. I was kind to each and every one of them. I am still a member to this day.

There is power in staying rooted in your purpose even when you are ignored. That does not mean it didn't sting you a little.

We are human and we feel hurt and disappointment.

There is a loneliness that comes with being strong. People assume strong women do not need encouragement. They assume confidence replaces vulnerability. They assume resilience eliminates the need for acknowledgment. That assumption is false.

Strength does not mean you don't feel. It means you feel deeply and keep going anyway.

There were days when I sat at tables by myself. Days when I walked into rooms knowing I would not be celebrated. Days when I realized that my presence would be tolerated but not embraced. In those moments, I had to make a choice. I could internalize their silence and let it erode my confidence. Or I could let their silence refine my self-validation.

I chose the second and eventually it no longer mattered. I dawned every door with a huge smile and hug for everyone. I learned how to clap for myself in rooms where no one else would. I continued to advertise all of my businesses everywhere no matter what. I learned how to honor my own accomplishments without waiting for permission. I learned how to sit alone without feeling lonely. I learned how to belong to myself first.

When people refuse to acknowledge you, it can trigger old wounds. Wounds of abandonment. Wounds of being overlooked. You fell underestimated and like you must prove your worth over and over again. We must train ourselves to transcend those feeling and no allow others that type of power over us.

That is not an easy lesson but I learned it. It made me even more appreciative of those that did come to me and quietly congratulate me. I focused on them and realized how blessed I was to have the few that would say the words.

But here is what I learned. Refusal to acknowledge you does

not mean you are insignificant. It often means you are not controllable.

Systems that reward conformity often feel threatened by authenticity. Groups built on hierarchy often resist independent thinkers. Environments that thrive on sameness rarely know what to do with leaders who move differently.

That is not your flaw. That is your power. I did not need their applause to keep building. I did not need their recognition to keep creating. I did not need their validation to keep impacting lives, and neither do you.

There will be places you outgrow while still being apart of them. There will be rooms where your spirit does not match the culture. There will be organizations you love that do not know how to love you back properly. I can sit in those rooms proudly now with no expectations whatsoever.

Everyone does not have to love or encourage you. That does not mean you leave your purpose. It means you strengthen your internal foundation. You go inside for what you need. You tell yourself everything you need to hear and you say it with conviction until you believe it.

I learned how to separate my mission from their acknowledgment. I trained myself to remain passionate about my duties without becoming bitter. I learned how to stay committed without becoming resentful. I knew how to be proud of myself even when others chose not to say it out loud.

That is emotional sovereignty. When you stop depending on external acknowledgment, you become unshakable. You stop performing. You stop explaining and seeking approval. You simply live, laugh, love and become who you were meant to be.

The most powerful thing I learned is this. The rooms that ignore you are not the rooms that define you. The silence of others does not cancel the voice of God within you.

My grandmother's legacy was not about being seen. It was about standing firm. It was about integrity. It was about showing up with purpose regardless of who was watching.

I stayed because I knew why I was there, and if you find yourself in a place where they refuse to acknowledge you, ask yourself this. Did you come for applause, or did you come for purpose?

If your answer is purpose, then keep standing. Keep smiling, Keep sitting at your own table. Keep building. Keep becoming who God destined you to be.

Because one day, the very thing they ignored will be the reason others find courage to stand on their own, and that is worth more than any recognition they could ever give you.

8

Acknowledge The Few

There comes a moment in life when you finally stop counting who didn't show up and start honoring who did. That moment changes everything. It is not loud. It is not dramatic. It is quiet, internal, and deeply freeing. It is the moment you realize that peace does not come from being supported by everyone, but from being fully present with the few who genuinely see you.

For a long time, I noticed who was missing. I noticed the silence. I noticed the lack of attention. I noticed who didn't call, didn't comment, didn't congratulate, didn't acknowledge. I told myself it didn't matter, but if I am being honest, it did. It mattered because I am human. Acknowledgment feels good. It mattered because when you pour your heart into your work, your healing, your growth, it is natural to want to be seen.

But one day, something shifted. I started noticing the people who never failed to show up. The ones who checked on me. The ones who drove me to the hospital when I had a tumor removed from my head in 2025. The ones who took the time to come by and visit while i recovered in bed for a entire month. The ones who sincerely celebrated my wins. The ones who supported me even when it was inconvenient. The ones who did not need to understand everything I was doing to believe in me. The ones who loved me without competition, comparison, or conditions. God had blessed me with many wonderful people in my life.

When I focused on them suddenly, the silence from everyone else grew faint. I once posted a simple motivational thought on Facebook that came straight from my spirit. It said something along the lines of this. "You should be so grateful and focused on the people who genuinely love and support you that you will not even notice the ones who don't." At the time, I didn't realize how true that statement would become in my own life.

When you begin to acknowledge the few, your emotional energy shifts. You stop scanning rooms for validation. and recognize the people who came all the way across the room just to hug you. You stop keeping mental tallies of who didn't clap and acknowledge all the beautiful warm smiles that sincerely greeted you.. You stop replaying moments of disappointment. Instead, you become grounded in appreciation and gratitude. You become rooted in reality. You become emotionally present.

The few are not random. They are divinely assigned, and that's priceless. They are the people who can celebrate you without feeling diminished. They do not feel threatened by your growth. They are the ones who can sit in your success without resentment. They are the ones who are not secretly hoping you fail so they can feel better about themselves.

Those people are rare, and because they are rare, they are priceless. We spend too much time mourning the crowd instead of protecting the circle. We think something is wrong because only a handful of people support us, but the truth is, that handful is exactly what keeps us sane, grounded, and protected. Not everyone deserves access to your journey. Not everyone deserves front row seats to your becoming. The older and wiser I become, the smaller my circle gets.

When you acknowledge the few, you stop romanticizing the many. I learned that the people who consistently support you are often the ones who have done their own inner work. They are emotionally mature enough to celebrate others. They are secure enough to clap without comparison. They are healed enough to love without envy, and those are the limited few you need in your corner.

Those are not common traits. That is why the few matter so much. There was a time when I thought something was wrong with me because I did not have massive support from every direction. Especially since I am naturally popular. I wondered why certain people remained distant. I wondered why others stayed quiet. I was concerned why some never acknowledged milestones that were significant to me.

Now I understand. It was never a reflection of my worth. It was a reflection of their capacity. People can only support you to the depth they support themselves. They can only celebrate you to the extent they believe in their own potential. People can only acknowledge you at the level of their emotional health. Wish them well and move forward.

Once I understood that it's not always about me, resentment faded. I stopped expecting people to give me what they did not have.

I stopped personalizing what was never personal. I stopped assigning meaning to their silence. Instead, I leaned into gratitude. I began to thank God for the few who consistently showed up for me. The ones who believed in me when it was not popular. The people who loved me when I was still figuring myself out.

ACKNOWLEDGE THE FEW

When I did that, something beautiful happened. My focus changed. When your focus changes, your emotions follow. I stopped feeling disappointed and started feeling supported. I stopped feeling overlooked and started feeling blessed. I no longer allowed myself to feel unappreciated and started feeling deeply grateful.

The few became more than enough. When you acknowledge the few, you also learn discernment. You learn that support does not always look loud. Some people support you with a simple hug and a smile. Some people pray for you privately. Some people root for you without public displays, and some people simply hold space for you to be yourself.

Support is not always a comment or a congratulatory message. Sometimes it is consistency. Sometimes it is presence. Simply picking up the phone when you call. Being a loyal friend or family member, or simply being that listening hear when you need one.

I learned to stop measuring support by noise and start recognizing it by behavior. Who shows up when it matters. Who celebrates without conditions and does not disappear when you elevate. Those are the few. Those are your life partners.

Once you truly acknowledge them, you become unfazed by everyone else. You stop seeking approval from people who were never meant to give it. No more chasing validation from spaces that were never safe for you. You stop hoping for recognition from people who are not rooting for you or anyone else for that matter. You begin to relax and take a breath and your nervous system calms. Your heart settles and your spirit strengthens. Because you know you are not alone. You know you are loved and supported by the people that are supposed to be in your life.

The truth is, being acknowledged by everyone would actually be overwhelming. It would blur your focus. It would dilute your purpose and invite opinions you do not need. It would expose you to energy that is not aligned with your growth.

The few protect you from that. They anchor and ground you. They remind you who you are when the noise of the world gets loud. When you acknowledge the few, you also learn humility. You realize that you do not need an audience to be impactful. You don't need a crowd to be significant. You were born worthy and you do not need widespread approval to be important.

You simply need alignment. You need authenticity. All you need peace and self-love. I have learned to internally thank the people who did not support me because their absence revealed who truly mattered. It made me stronger. Their silence created space for deeper connections and spiritual growth. Their lack of acknowledgment pushed me inward, where I found my own voice.

Once you find that voice, everything changes. You stop needing permission, and you stop waiting for love and recognition. There is no more explaining who you are and why you are valuable. You move forward in your life with clarity and certainty, no matter who agrees.

You realize that life was never meant to be lived for applause. It was meant to be lived with purpose. Focus on what god put you on this earth to do and no longer allow the approval of other people to distract you from that.

Walking in your purpose does not require a crowd. It requires courage. It requires the deepest, unshakable self-love. It requires gratitude for all that you have been blessed with.

So if you find yourself disappointed by the lack of support from some people, pause, take a deep breath. Look in the mirror and remember who you are. You are Great and this is your life to create.

There are people in your life who see you, love you, and support you in ways you may have overlooked. They may not be many, but they are enough. Respect and honor them. Give thanks for them. Protect those relationships. Let them matter more than the silence of others.

Because when you truly acknowledge the few that love and support you, you become immune to the rejection of others. You become grounded in love. You become emotionally free, and that freedom is worth more than all the applause in the world.

Pep Rally at Centennial High School in Compton Ca 1986-87

9

When Your Validation Becomes Internal

There is a moment in every healing journey that does not come with fireworks, applause, or announcements. It comes quietly and internally. It happens when you realize you are still checking the room. You have begun the healing but you are still scanning faces for approval. Still wondering who noticed, and hoping someone will say what you already know is true. That moment is subtle, but it is powerful.

For a long time, I did not realize how often I was looking over my shoulder. Not physically, but emotionally. I would accomplish something meaningful like writing a new book or starting a new business, and immediately wonder who noticed, who was proud of me. I would do something brave and instinctively check for a reaction. I would make progress and feel proud for a split second, only to look outward to see if that pride was reflected back to me. I did not recognize this as dependency at the time. I thought it was normal. I thought it was human. I thought it meant I cared. I had operated this was for many years as a young woman. I needed approval from sisters, God-mothers and friends.

WHEN YOUR VALIDATION BECOMES INTERNAL

But caring is not the same as needing confirmation. You can care enough to want to share whats new and exciting in your life but your plans can't change because someone close to you does not agree.

Looking over your shoulder becomes a habit when your sense of worth was shaped in environments where love felt uncertain and conditional. When praise came inconsistently and approval felt like safety. You learn to measure your value by the response of others and that is not OK. Many of us listen for applause before our trust your own footing. When you continue this way, before you know it, you find yourself living your life with one eye on your path and the other on the people you need to be in agreement with the path you chose..

That is exhausting. I definitely got tired of living that way. There came a season in my life when I noticed how much energy I was spending monitoring reactions. Who liked what I posted or took the time to acknowledged what I achieved. I was still noticing who said nothing. I told myself I was just observant. I told myself I was intuitive and aware. But the truth was simpler and harder to accept. I was still waiting to be chosen emotionally. Inside I was still anxious and needy.

When you are constantly checking for response, you are not fully in your life. You can't even enjoy your own success because you are half in your purpose and half in other people's opinions. You are half grounded and half reaching. You are half confident and half unsure. That divided posture affects how you move, how you speak, how you decide, and how you trust yourself.

The shift began when I asked myself a difficult question. If no one ever clapped again, would I still do this? If no one acknowledged this version of me, would I still show up as her? If no one affirmed my growth, would I still honor it?

At first, the answer scared me. Because honesty revealed how much I was still depending on external reinforcement to fuel internal belief. That realization was not comfortable, but it was necessary.

When you stop looking over your shoulder, you stop living in fragments. You begin to live whole.

This does not mean you stop appreciating encouragement. It does not mean you become cold or detached or ungrateful. It means encouragement becomes a bonus, not a requirement. It means validation becomes welcomed, not awaited. It means support becomes appreciated, not chased.

There is a profound difference between enjoying applause and needing it.

I began practicing something intentionally. I stopped announcing certain wins. I stopped explaining myself unnecessarily. I stopped justifying my decisions to people who had no authority over my life. I stopped looking for permission to feel proud. I stopped seeking reassurance for choices that already felt aligned in my spirit.

At first, it felt uncomfortable. Silence can feel loud when you are used to noise. Peace can feel unfamiliar when you are used to reaction. But slowly, something beautiful happened. I started hearing myself more clearly. My intuition grew stronger. My confidence became quieter but deeper. I felt less reactive and more rooted.

When you stop looking over your shoulder, you realize how much weight you were carrying that was never yours to hold.

You were never meant to manage people's expectations of you. It is not your job to police their emotions. It is time to stop attempting to convince others of your worth. That work is too heavy and too unnecessary. The moment you release it, your shoulders drop. Your breath deepens. Your decisions sharpen. Your peace expands. You are already enough, its time to accept that.

I noticed something else too. The people who truly loved me did not require me to perform for them. They did not need constant updates. They did not need proof that I was productive. They see my daily hustle. They see how I constantly encourage others daily, and that is great but in the end even if someone does not notice you keep going. You keep creating and developing into the wonderful person you were made to be.

It is time to stop looking over your shoulder, stop letting other people define you. You stay on your path toward greatness no longer interpret lack of response as lack of value. You no longer confuse quiet with rejection. Let people be quiet and never say the words of encouragement you need. Become someone who does not need that. Give it to yourself. Create daily habits that uplift you. Look at yourself daily in the mirror and remind yourself that you matter most. Speak positive affirmations to yourself repeatedly until you believe them.

Learn to shift your confidence from external to internal. Love yourself from the inside out. Become your own best friend.

I began to understand that not everyone is meant to witness your transformation. Some people only knew the version of you that made them feel better about themselves. When you outgrow that version, they no longer recognize you. That does not mean you are wrong. It means you are evolving. We all have the opportunity to intentionally evolve into better, stronger and more successful people. However the decision to do so should be made because you desire it, it can not be made to impress others.

True growth and transformations begins inside of us. Growth

does not need a witness. There is a sacred kind of power that comes from doing the work in private. From healing quietly and building without announcements. From evolving without permission.

The more I stopped looking over my shoulder, the more I began to depend on myself for encouragement. I was no longer willing to edit my joy to fit other people's comfort. How often I had dimmed my pride to avoid being misunderstood was unfortunate. How often I had waited for someone else to validate moments that were already meaningful was sad but it was over.

That waiting delayed my peace and my pride. I had always been worthy. I was a successful business owner and a great asset to the community. i did not need anyone to cheer for me. I had worked hard to become the determined entrepreneur that I was.

I want everyone reading this book to realize that you do not need a witness to honor your progress. You do not need an audience to celebrate your healing. there is no need for someone else's agreement to move forward in your life. You should be proud of yourself no matter what.

When you stop expecting support from others, you stop outsourcing your confidence.

That is where true freedom lives. That is where authentic self-esteems are built. Whatever you accomplish be proud of yourself. Even when ideas fail, still be proud that you tried.

This chapter is not about isolation. It is about independence. Emotional independence. Spiritual independence. The kind that allows you to stand steady regardless of who shows up. The kind that allows you to feel whole regardless of who claps for you.

This is the space where you stop performing and start being comfortable with just yourself, your choices and your decisions. Where you stop chasing the reaction of others and start trusting

WHEN YOUR VALIDATION BECOMES INTERNAL

your own direction. This is where you stop waiting to be affirmed and start affirming yourself.

This is the moment that you **Become Your Own Cheerleader.**

10

Becoming the Voice You Needed

Early on in life, I learned not to expect support from people. I didn't learn it gently. I learned it through silence. Through moments where I stood proud of myself, only to be met with indifference. Through milestones that felt monumental to me, but ordinary to the people I thought would celebrate them. I was too young to understand that silence doesn't always mean disapproval, and I was too young not to take it personally. So I did what many of us do. I internalized it. I assumed something was wrong with me.

At that age, I believed support was proof of worth. I thought love showed up loudly and people who loved you showed you with their cheers of pride and acknowledgment. I believed if people didn't cheer, it meant I wasn't doing enough, or that I was not smart enough. I felt it meant I wasn't good enough or maybe not as successful as I thought I was. What I didn't know then was that some people don't know how to celebrate what they've never allowed themselves to become. It would be years before I realized that their lack of support was not about me at all. It was about them. I could no longer concern myself with them.

Inside of them may have been a missing puzzle piece that I had already found in me. many people want success but never took that leap of faith. Without doing so, they simply could not support me, because doing so would have forced them to confront everything they never chased or never tried. To them, I looked like I was always winning. I was always re-inventing myself and starting a new business. What they couldn't see was the emotional trauma that drove me. They didn't see the fear I carried for years. The grief I felt for those I lost in life. The exhaustion from sustaining a business for thirty years. The moments where I wanted to quit but didn't feel like I was allowed to. They saw the outcome, not the struggle.

There is a particular loneliness that comes from being strong too early in life. From becoming capable before you ever felt safe. Learning how to encourage yourself before you ever learned how to heal from all you had been through. When you grow up like that, you don't just move forward alone, you learn how to talk to yourself in the quiet and coach yourself through disappointment. You learn how to clap for yourself in rooms where no one else notices. While that skill eventually becomes a superpower, at first, it feels like abandonment. It is not always that, but that is what it feels like.

There is a degree of wisdom you gain after you lived long enough. Eventually you begin to understand and realize, that it is not always personal or about you. It is a lot of hurt people in this world that are simply dealing with there own mess. I had to understand that many people had suffered through tragedies just like me. Everyone has not began the journey of healing yet. Most don't even know how to begin that journey.

I remember wishing someone would say, "I see you SaBrina." I absolutely needed validation from others in my younger years. I needed to know that my efforts mattered, and that someone noticed. I needed to know that the weight I was carrying wasn't invisible. But the truth is, no one can validate pain they've never even allowed themselves to feel. No one can cheer for a journey they're too afraid to take themselves.

That realization changed everything for me. I stopped waiting for people to become who they were never equipped to be. I no longer had expectations of them uplifting me. I stopped handing out emotional microphones and hoping someone else would speak life into me. Instead I learn to speak that life into myself. I began to understand that what I was searching for externally was something I had to build internally. I needed to become the voice I once searched for in others.

Becoming that voice didn't happen overnight. It came in pieces, in stages. There were many moments of self-doubt where I chose encouragement instead of criticism. My transformation came in seasons. I talked to myself like I would a child learning how to walk. Gently. Patiently. Honestly. I re-trained my mind to know that I was valuable. I stopped berating myself for being unwanted by my mother. I stopped shaming myself for being abandoned. I stopped pretending that those facts did not hurt me, because they did.

I learned how to say, "I'm proud of you Bri," even when no one else said it first. That was the beginning of something sacred. There is a difference between confidence and self-trust. Self-trust is built on consistency with yourself. Tell yourself great things about yourself until you believe them. Be repetitive until those positive words become second nature and they seep into your subconscious.

When you become the voice you needed, you stop allowing others to determine your worth. You stop allowing silence to define your value. You begin to understand that support is not always withheld from you out of malice. Sometimes it's withheld out of incapacity.

Some people simply cannot give what they never received, and that is not your fault. Once I accepted that truth, I stopped shrinking to make others comfortable. I no longer explained my dreams to people who only understood survival. I stopped looking for mirrors in rooms full of windows. I learned how to speak to myself in a way that kept me moving forward, even when no one was walking beside me.

I became my own reminder on the hard days. It was me who gave myself reassurance on the uncertain days. I became my own witness, and here's what no one tells you about becoming that voice: it doesn't make you cold, although it may seem that way at times. It makes you responsible. It teaches you how to create a relationship with the inner you, the spiritual you. It may seem like it makes you distant but in actuality it makes you more discerning. Once you release resentment for those who just won't say the words, you develop and peace and you no longer need any ones support but your own.

When you stop begging for other peoples encouragement, you start building the endurance needed to tackle anything in this world. Yes sometimes it can make you sad and it can feel lonely, but I assure you if you continue to do the mental, emotional and spiritual work on yourself that pain and loneliness will subside.

I want to speak directly to the woman reading this who has done more than she's ever been acknowledged for. The one who shows up even when she's tired. The one who carries responsibility quietly and has learned how to survive on minimal praise. You were right, they ignored you. You didn't imagine the absence of support. You felt it because it was indeed real. But it did not diminish who you are. It refined you. It prepared you for a world where you simply have to uplift yourself at times. You must cheer for yourself.

The lack of support did not happen because you weren't worthy. You are worthy and I want each of you to be very proud of yourself. You were unsupported because you were becoming something unfamiliar to others. Something that held a mirror to people who could not look at themselves. People are comfortable clapping for what fits inside their realm of understanding. Growth often doesn't.

Becoming the voice you needed means learning how to validate your own experience without needing agreement. It means trusting your inner knowing even when it contradicts the opinions around you. It means choosing to speak life into yourself on days when the world is silent.

It also means grieving. Grieving the version of yourself that waited on others to build your self worth. It is time to grieve and let go of the childhood moments where encouragement would have changed everything for you. It's time to let go of the belief that love and support always shows up the way we need it to. Believing and needing that is not weakness. It is honesty, and honesty is where healing begins.

At some point, I realized that the reason I could encourage others so deeply was because I had practiced on myself in the mirror so much. The reason my words carried weight was because they had carried me when I needed to be lifted up. I could recognize resilience in others was because I had lived it, and continue to live it to this day.

That's when I understood something powerful: the voice I became was shaped by necessity, but it became a gift. It is my super power and you have one too.

You don't become your own cheerleader because it's trendy. You become it because life demands it. Because waiting on others can cost you time and peace of mind. Because shrinking to stay supported can cost you purpose. Because silence can either break you or build you up, depending on what you do with it.

When you learn how to encourage yourself, you stop fearing isolation. You stop seeing solitude as rejection. You start recognizing it as preparation for the real world and whatever it brings you.

You become unshakeable, not because life stops shaking you, but because you know how to stay focused even in the midst of chaos.

Here's the most important part: becoming the voice you needed doesn't mean you no longer value support. Sincere, positive support is a blessing. It means you are no longer dependent on it. It means you can receive encouragement without requiring it. It means you can appreciate applause without chasing them. You no longer crumble without them.

You move differently when you know who you are, regardless of who is watching. So if you've ever felt overlooked, unheard, or unsupported, know this: you are not alone and that pain will pass and turn into fuel to propel you into a great future. The voice you built inside of yourself will carry you farther than applause ever could. One day, someone will hear you speak with conviction and wonder how you became so sure of yourself.

They will never see the nights you had to be your own comfort.

They will never hear the conversations you had with yourself just to keep going. But you will know, and you will take comfort in that. Because you didn't just survive the silence of others. You learned how to speak life into it. You became the voice you needed and you never looked back.

11

No Need to Confront

There was a season in my life when I believed confrontation was the cure for disappointment. I truly thought that if I could just explain myself clearly enough, express my hurt honestly enough, or articulate my feelings passionately enough, the other person would finally understand. I believed that once they knew how much they had disappointed me, something inside of them would shift. I believed accountability would bring connection and honesty would bring healing. I was wrong.

I was a little hurt firecracker when I was younger. Mad at the world and willing to confront anyone who said something I did not like. What I did not understand then is that confrontation does not automatically lead to clarity, and it certainly does not guarantee compassion. Fortunately it did not lead to any physical fights but it very well could have. I was so hurt by the cards that life had dealt me, that I did not really care.

Most often confrontation does not bring peace, nor does it resolve matters. Sometimes it brings satisfaction to the very people who never intended to support you in the first place. It lets them know they mattered enough to wound you. It confirms that their actions of lack their of had power over you. As hard as this truth is to swallow, some people simply do not care that they hurt you. Some people are unmoved by your pain and do not want reconciliation. They want reaction. that is exactly what i used to give them.

That realization alone will mature you faster than anything else., or at least it should.

When I was younger, I confronted everything and everybody. I confronted people who disappointed me. I confronted people who ignored me. I confronted people who did not clap when I thought they should have. I confronted people who looked the other way while I was showing up fully and authentically. I confronted family and friends, because I thought nipping things in the bud would keep me from being hurt.

Almost every time, I walked away feeling worse. Not because I was wrong for expressing myself, but because I was giving emotional access to people who did not deserve it. I was opening my heart to people who had already shown me through their behavior that they were not safe with my vulnerability. I was explaining my pain to people who benefited from my confusion.

And to be honest, I often looked emotional. I looked reactive. I looked like I cared more than they did. I looked like I was begging to be understood. And there is nothing empowering about that position.

One of the most humbling lessons of maturity is realizing that not every disappointment requires a conversation. Not every hurt deserves an explanation. Every offense needs to be addressed. Some people understand you perfectly. They just do not care. That truth hurts, but it also frees you.

At some point, I had to ask myself a hard question. Is this confrontation going to lead to love, or is it going to lead to more pain? Am I coming to them in love or control? Is this conversation going to bring peace, or is it going to feed my ego's need to be acknowledged? Am I speaking because there is potential for growth, or am I speaking because I want them to know they hurt me?

It took years for me to get there but becoming mature enough to ask myself those questions changed everything for me. I began to understand that negative confrontation is not about courage at all. It is about fear. Just because you can confront does not mean you should. Just because you have the words does not mean they need to be spoken. Growth bring emotional intelligence.

As I matured, I learned a simple personal rule. If I cannot confront from a place of calm, clarity, and love, I leave it alone. If I do not believe the other person has the capacity to receive what I am saying without defensiveness, anger, or retaliation, I let it go. If I sense that the conversation will turn into justification, denial, or emotional warfare, I choose peace instead. Most importantly, if I will be emotionally effected by their response, it is best to let it go.

This is not weakness. This is wisdom. There is power in restraint and wisdom in silence. There is maturity in choosing yourself over the need to be heard by people who are not listening anyway.

Each day that passes without confrontation, is positive growth. The charge weakens when you take a breath and think first. The attachment to what you were so hurt or upset about subsides. You realize you are not as emotionally hurt as you thought you were. You realize your life continues, and your peace matters more than their awareness.

That does not mean you become passive or voiceless. It means you become selective. There are moments when confrontation is necessary, but it still should be done calmly and without anger. There are moments when boundaries must be spoken. Times will come when silence would be self betrayal. You do have to stick up for yourself at times. I am not suggesting you swallow disrespect or ignore harm. I am saying discernment must lead the decision.

If you believe there is a genuine chance that a conversation can bring understanding, mutual respect, and love, then I would initiate that conversation. If you believe the person is emotionally mature enough to hear you without turning it into a battlefield, then it's OK to have that conversation. If you think the relationship is valuable enough to fight for in a healthy way, then attempt to speak.

But if the confrontation is only going to drain you, diminish you, or destabilize your peace, you should choose yourself. Learning to make that choice took me years to learn.

I used to believe that explaining myself or asking others to explain themselves to me was strength. Now I understand that protecting my energy is strength. I used to believe being honest meant being loud. Now I understand that being honest sometimes means walking away quietly. I used to believe confrontation proved confidence. Now I understand that type of confidence often shows up as indifference.

When you stop confronting people who do not support you, something shifts inside of you. You stop needing them to validate your experience. You stop waiting for them to change. You stop hoping for an apology that may never come. You no longer give them free rent in your emotional space. You learn to redirect that energy inward.

This is where becoming your own cheerleader truly begins.

Instead of rehearsing conversations that will never happen, you start investing in yourself mentally and emotionally. No more crafting speeches in your head, instead you begin building your life and preparing your future for success. You no longer feel the need to prove your worth to others, instead you start living in alignment with it.

You learn that peace is louder than confrontation. Growth is more valuable than explanation. Inner healing is more important than reaction.

The most powerful realization of all is this. You do not need people to understand you in order to move forward. You do not need their acknowledgment to be valid. You do not need their support to succeed in your life. All you need your own.

There will always be people who watch you grow silently. There will always be people who benefit from your presence without celebrating your progress. Your job is not to educate them on how to love you. Your job is to love yourself enough to stop chasing what is not being offered.

When you no longer confront every disappointment, you conserve your emotional currency. You become more intentional and less reactive. You become grounded and stable. You become unbothered in the healthiest way.

Eventually, you realize something profound. The people who truly matter never required confrontation in the first place. They showed up with support and love.

They spoke up for you even when you weren't there. They clapped without being asked, and they supported you without being reminded.

Everyone else was simply revealing where they belonged in your life.

No confrontation required. That is not avoidance. That's

growth and evolution.

12

Standing Ovation: Live Like You Believe in You

There comes a moment when the applause you once waited for no longer matters. You don't need them anymore. Not because you no longer care, but because you finally understand something deeper. You were never meant to live your life waiting to be affirmed by the people around you. You were meant to live your life rooted, steady, and confident in who you are, regardless of who claps.

A standing ovation is not something you receive. It is something you give to yourself. For most of my life, I thought this wonderful feeling came after validation. I thought confidence was built when others confirmed it. I assumed worth was something you earned once enough people recognized it. But life taught me otherwise. Slowly and sometimes painfully I learned that other peoples opinion of you has absolutely nothing to do with you. Their opinion of you should have no effect on how you feel about yourself.

Living like you believe in you means you stop waiting for permission to take your place in the world. It means you stop shrinking your truth so others feel comfortable around you. You stop second guessing the very instincts that carried you this far. It means you will no longer apologize for your resilience, your growth, your strength, and your survival. I'm sure it was not easy to get this far in life. I know it wasn't for me. But I did it. I succeeded and so can you.

It is time to take control of how you speak to yourself when no one is listening. When you are alone with yourself make a conscious choice to empower yourself. Make it your responsibility to encourage yourself. The quality of the life you live depends on it.

This is what separates those who burn out from those who rise. Not necessarily talent. Not even opportunity and definitely not luck. But strong belief in yourself that is not dependent on external reinforcement.

I had to learn how to clap for myself and I pray each one of you learns the same. It was vital for me to learn how to honor my own milestones and stop expecting others to acknowledge them. I had to learn how to be happy with my accomplishments without immediately wondering who noticed them. That did not come naturally. It came getting tired of being let down by other and finally realizing that I was strong enough and powerful enough to encourage myself.

There is something incredibly powerful about waking up each day and moving like you already believe in you. It's extremely liberating. There is no feeling like it. When you realize that you are all you need you make decisions differently. you get up with a different zest for life in the mornings. You got you and that is enough.

Living like you believe in you does not mean you never feel hurt. It means hurt does not debilitate you. It means disappointment no longer derails you. Rejection no longer has the power to dismantles your confidence. You still feel everything fully but you do not let it consume you.

You learn how to hold your head high even when your heart feels tender. You keep your posture strong even when your spirit is tired. You walk forward without dragging the weight of other people's approval behind you.

A standing ovation is earned through endurance and consistency. You have earned it by showing up again after being overlooked. By choosing integrity over popularity. You have honored your path even when it was lonely and exhausting. You believed in your calling even when others doubted it.

Some of the strongest people you will ever meet learned how to cheer for themselves. I may have learn to cheer for others by being on the cheerleading squad in High School, but life has taught me to become my own personal cheerleader.

I want you to understand something important. You are an amazing human being with limitless potential. No matter what you have been through or what mistakes you may have made in life, as long as you have breath in your body, you can become whoever you want to be in life. But do it for yourself, not to impress others. Some of the most meaningful work happens unseen. Some of the greatest transformations occur without witnesses. Many of the strongest victories are celebrated internally before they are ever acknowledged publicly.

Your life does not need an audience to be valid. When you live like you believe in you, you stop needing constant reassurance. You got this, so stop asking for confirmation. Stop waiting for green lights from people who are standing still. You trust your own timing. Trust your own instincts. You trust your own growth.

Living like you believe in you also means releasing resentment. It means letting go of the anger you held toward people who could not show up for you. Try to understand that some people simply do not have the capacity to clap because they are still struggling to strive for themselves. Pray for them and release them of the responsibility of uplifting you. You can do that for yourself now.

Live like you believe in you when you walk into rooms. Walk in with your head held high because you are a valuable and capable human being. Let today be the last day that you speak lack and limitation over your own life because you are great and it's time to remember that.

This book was never about teaching you how to force applause. It was about teaching you how to stop needing them from others. It was about reminding you that your worth was never up for debate. It was about guiding you back to your true self.

The loudest standing ovation you will ever receive will not come from a crowd. It will come from within you. It will come the moment you realize you no longer need to be seen to be significant. You are already significant.

So stand tall. Breathe deep. Laugh loud, Love hard and Live like you believe in you. Because you do.

Me and my Friend Danette 1978 – Centennial High School in Compton Ca

About the Author

SaBrina Fisher Reece understands what it means to keep going without applause.

For over twenty-six years, she built one of the most influential braiding salons and schools in Los Angeles-**Braids By SaBrina**-earning recognition throughout California as "The Braid Queen." Her name was on the door, her reputation on the line, and her success was self-made. But behind the achievements was a quieter truth: much of her journey was navigated without consistent support, validation, or encouragement from others.

Become Your Own Cheerleader: Moving Forward in Life Without the Support of Others is born from that reality.

In this deeply personal book, SaBrina shares the internal work required to stand strong when no one is clapping, to lead without external affirmation, and to keep believing in yourself even when the room is silent. Though she once served as her high school varsity cheerleading captain, literally cheering for others, this book explores a different kind of cheer: the inner discipline of self-belief, emotional resilience, and self-approval.

SaBrina's life has been shaped by early abandonment, profound loss, and hard-earned self-trust. Those experiences taught her that confidence on the outside does not always mean peace on the inside, and that real strength is learned when you are forced to become your own support system.

Today, SaBrina is an author, speaker, and guide focused on emotional growth, self-mastery, and inner alignment. She is the author of several transformational works, including *My Spiritual Smile, Your Mind Is Magic, Perfectly Positive, Living Life on a Higher Frequency, How to Get Exactly What You Want From God, Kicking Depression in the Butt, When I Say "I Am", and How to Make More Money in 2026*. Each reflects a chapter of her own evolution.

Now residing in New Mexico, SaBrina continues her work through writing, sound-based healing practices and helping others bring their literary dreams to print through **In59Seconds Publishing Co.** She is always reminding readers that there is no single path to peace, only the courage to walk your own.

Her message is simple and unwavering:

Sometimes the most important applause you will ever receive is the one you give yourself.

You can connect with me on:

- https://in59secondspublishing.com
- https://www.facebook.com/BraidQueenSaBrinaReece

Also by SaBrina Fisher Reece

SaBrina Fisher Reece is a transformational author, speaker, and spiritual guide whose work centers on healing, mindset, and purposeful living. She is best known for her decades-long career as the owner of **Braids By SaBrina**, a groundbreaking salon and school in Los Angeles that became a cultural landmark and empowered generations through artistry and entrepreneurship.

After more than thirty years in the beauty industry, SaBrina felt called to share the inner journey behind her success, one shaped by faith, resilience, and personal transformation. Her writing reflects her lived experience and spiritual awakening, offering readers practical tools for emotional healing, positive thinking, and inner peace.

She is the author of **My Spiritual Smile, Kicking Depression in the Butt, Family Fun Night Cookbook, Your Mind Is Magic, Perfectly Positive, Living Life on a Higher Frequency, When I Say " I AM"** and other works devoted to self-discovery and empowerment.

Now based in the beautiful "Land of Enchantment" New Mexico, SaBrina continues to help others create their literary legacy through In59Seconds Publishing Co. She is and will always be writing, speaking, offering sound vibration sessions, incorporating crystal bowls, tuning forks, and frequency-based practices. Above all, she believes there is no single path to healing, only the sacred journey each person takes to reconnect with their own divine power.

One of her most popular saying is: You are Great and this is Your Life to Create - So Lets Go!

How To Make More Money In 2026

How to Make More Money in 2026: Creating Residual Income from Your Home is a motivational, step-by-step mindset and money guide for everyday people who are ready to stop surviving and start building. This is not "get rich quick." This is "get focused, get aligned, and get paid for what you already know."

Inside, SaBrina Fisher Reece walks you through the real shift that changes everything: the new wealth mindset for 2026. Because before money shows up in your account, it has to show up in your thinking. You'll learn how to move from scarcity to strategy, how to turn your skills into real income streams, and how to build income that keeps working even when you are resting.

This book breaks down how residual income is created through digital products, smart systems, automation, branding, and consistent cash flow habits that don't require a fancy background or a perfect life. You'll learn how to monetize what you already know, package your value, and build from your home with the tools you already have.

What makes this book different is the voice behind it. SaBrina built her life through entrepreneurship, and she shares the truth from experience. After decades of running a successful salon and becoming an author, she launched In59Seconds Publishing Company from her computer at home, at her cute little pink desk, proving that reinvention is possible at any age and any stage. If she can learn it, you can learn it too.

If you're ready to make 2026 the year you stop watching other people win, and start building a legacy from your living room, this book is for you.

You don't need permission. You need a decision.

Small Business Basics

Small Business Basics is the powerful story of how a young woman with no blueprint, no support, and no safety net built one of Los Angeles' most recognized braid studios—and the step-by-step guide she created so others could rise too.

Through raw honesty and decades of wisdom, SaBrina Fisher Reece reveals the lessons that shaped her journey: how to start before you're ready, how to visualize success, how to market with courage, how to lead with compassion, how to set boundaries, and how to build a business that reflects your purpose—not your past.

This book blends practical business strategies with personal growth, healing, and spiritual insight, reminding readers that entrepreneurship is not just about making money—it's about becoming the strongest version of yourself. If you're ready to build a business rooted in discipline, faith, confidence, and heart, this book will show you the way.

Your Mind Is Magic

How to Get Exactly What You Want From God shows you how to pray with results. Inside, you'll learn how to make specific requests, build the faith needed to sustain them, and match your thoughts and emotions to the outcome you want. SaBrina teaches you how to interrupt negative self-talk, eliminate doubt, and step into a mindset that attracts divine answers quickly and clearly. This is your guide to intentional prayer, spiritual alignment, and receiving blessings without hesitation.

Living Life on a Higher Frequency

Living Life on a Higher Frequency is your road map to emotional peace, spiritual clarity, and magnetic abundance. In this transformative guide, SaBrina Fisher Reece shows you how simple, intentional shifts in your thoughts, habits, and daily awareness can elevate your vibration and reshape every area of your life. With wisdom rooted in experience and teachings anchored in universal spiritual law, she reveals how your inner frequency determines the quality of your relationships, your opportunities, your joy, and even your ability to manifest the life you truly desire.

If you're ready to release emotional heaviness, interrupt limiting beliefs, reclaim your power, and step into a higher state of alignment, this book will show you the path. SaBrina gently guides you toward a life where peace becomes your default, intuition becomes your compass, and abundance becomes your natural state of being.

Whether you are healing, growing, or awakening to your next level, **Living Life on a Higher Frequency** will help you rise with intention, clarity, and confidence. If you're ready to feel lighter, think clearer, love deeper, and ascend into the most empowered version of yourself—your journey starts here.

When I Say "I AM"

What you say after "I Am" has the power to shape your entire life.

In *When I Say "I Am"*, SaBrina Fisher Reece reveals the sacred and scientific power of spoken identity. Blending spiritual truth, biblical wisdom, and universal law, this transformational book teaches readers how their words are not just communication, but creation. Every "I Am" statement becomes a command to the subconscious, a signal to the universe, and a declaration to the spiritual realm.

Drawing from scripture, including God's revelation of "I AM" as the eternal source of being, SaBrina shows how the same creative force lives within each of us. Through emotionally moving insight, practical affirmations, and deep spiritual awareness, readers learn how to shift from fear-based language to faith-based declarations that activate healing, confidence, abundance, and purpose.

This book will help you:

Break negative identity patterns

Reprogram limiting beliefs

Speak life instead of fear

Align your words with divine promise

Use "I Am" as a daily tool for transformation

More than motivation, *When I Say "I Am"* is a blueprint for conscious creation. It reminds you that your voice is powerful, your identity is sacred, and your words are always working, either for you or against you.

If you are ready to stop speaking survival and start speaking destiny, this book will show you how to command your life with intention, faith, and divine authority, one "I Am" at a time.

Kicking Depression in the Butt

Kicking Depression in the Butt is a raw, faith-infused, and deeply practical guide for anyone who is tired of surviving in silence and ready to reclaim their life.

Drawing from her own lived experiences with trauma, abandonment, loss, and depression, SaBrina Fisher Reece invites readers into an honest conversation about what depression really feels like, and how to fight back. This book does not minimize pain or offer shallow positivity. Instead, it helps readers recognize depression as an internal enemy, interrupt destructive thought cycles, and rebuild their inner world with intention, truth, and daily tools that actually work.

Through personal storytelling, spiritual insight, and mindset-shifting strategies, SaBrina shows readers how to stop identifying with their darkest thoughts and begin designing a life that protects their peace. She addresses the realities of trauma, triggers, boundaries, faith, therapy, medication, and personal responsibility, offering a balanced approach that honors both professional support and inner work.

Kicking Depression in the Butt is for the person who keeps showing up while quietly falling apart. It is for those who smile while suffering, who feel strong on the outside but exhausted on the inside. Most of all, it is a reminder that depression may visit, but it does not get to stay, and it does not get to become your identity.

This book is not about perfection. It's about progress. It's about learning how to fight for your mind, your peace, and your future, one thought, one choice, and one day at a time.

Because as long as you have breath in your body, your story is not over, and you still have the power to kick depression in the butt.

www.ingramcontent.com/pod-product-compliance
Lightning Source LLC
LaVergne TN
LVHW021714080426
835510LV00010B/1001